PIERRE BERTON RESOURCE LIBRARY
4921 Rutherford Road
Woodbridge, Ontario   L4L 1A6

JAN 2 9 2008

VAUGHAN PUBLIC

D1237870

J
388.
09
Gal

Galford, Ellen.

Transportation

PICTURE THAT!

TRANSPORTATION
By Land, Sea & Air

EXPLORING HISTORY through ART

ELLEN GALFORD

MINNETONKA, MINNESOTA

Copyright © 2007 Two-Can Publishing and Toucan Books Ltd.

Two-Can Publishing
11571 K-Tel Drive
Minnetonka, MN 55343
www.two-canpublishing.com

Editorial Director: Jill Anderson

Created by
Toucan Books Ltd.
3rd Floor
89 Charterhouse Street
London EC1M 6HR

Project Manager: Ellen Dupont
Art Director: Bradbury and Williams
Editor: Theresa Bebbington
Designer: Bob Burroughs
Proofreader: Marion Dent
Indexer: Michael Dent
Picture Researcher: Christine Vincent
Author: Ellen Galford
Series Consultant: David Wilkins

All rights reserved. No part of this work covered on the copyrights herein may be reproduced or used in any form or by any means—graphic, electronic, or mechanical, including photocopying, recording, and taping of information on storage and retrieval systems—without the prior written permission of the publisher.

ISBN 978-1-58728-590-5

Library of Congress Catalog Card Number : 2007007323

1 2 3 4 5 11 10 09 08 07

Printed in Singapore

CONTENTS

TRAVEL ON LAND

UNTIL THE MID-1800S, TRAVEL ON LAND RELIED ON MUSCLE POWER.
MOST PEOPLE TRAVELED ONLY AS FAR AS THEY COULD WALK. OTHERS
RODE ON HORSEBACK OR IN VEHICLES PULLED BY OXEN OR HORSES.

PICTURE THIS! THE YEAR IS 1895. You live in a small town in North America. It is only 25 miles (40 km) from a big city, but it might as well be in another world. No one from your family has ever been there.

There are only three streets in your town, and none of them is paved. When it rains, they turn into a horrible mass of mud, churned up by horses' hooves and wagon wheels. No matter the weather, everybody is careful crossing Main Street, where there are always piles of horse manure. The ladies have to lift the hems of their long skirts to avoid them.

The place where you live is too small to have a railroad station of its own, but train tracks run through the fields a few miles from your house.

THE BICYCLE APPEARED in the 1860s. This pedal-powered riding machine was known as a velocipede (or "fast foot"). Long skirts got tangled in the wheels, so women riders wore pantaloons instead.

There have been trains running through this part of the country for 30 years now, bringing people to settle in the West. Your parents remember when the trains first arrived.

When you lie in bed at night you can hear the whistle of a locomotive. It is a lonely sound, and it makes you wonder about the people riding the trains and the faraway places they might be going. However, you can't stay awake for too long. You have to get up early to make it to school on time. The schoolhouse is two miles (3 km) away, and you have to walk. Even in pouring rain or blowing snow, there is no other way for you to get there.

Your family does not own a horse. Even if your parents could afford to feed such a large animal,

IN 1673, MESSENGERS ON HORSEBACK *began carrying mail between Boston and New York. As settlers pushed westward, stagecoaches became more popular for transporting mailbags—and passengers. In the mid-1800s, such journeys were long and uncomfortable. The trip from Memphis, Tennessee, to San Francisco took 25 days—and much longer in bad weather.*

they hardly need one. Your father, like your neighbors, works in town. He walks to his job at the blacksmith's shop. Your mother walks to the general store every day to buy food and supplies. The store sells fresh produce, meat, and eggs from the local farmers. If your mother wants something heavy, such as a big sack of flour, the storekeeper will deliver it to your home in his horse-drawn cart.

One person who does own a fast horse is the town doctor. He knows that patients might die if he cannot reach them in time. Then one day he amazes everybody by driving down Main Street in a horseless carriage. Everyone has heard of this new invention, but no one has seen one. It is a noisy machine and sends the dogs into a frenzy of barking. Horses rear up in panic. The future has arrived.

EVERY RAILROAD wanted people to travel on their trains. Colorful posters were used to let them know about new train services. This 1874 poster is for the Erie Railway, based in Chicago, Illinois.

A DAY AT THE FAIR

FOR THE PEOPLE ENJOYING THIS COUNTRY FAIR near London, England, horses are the center of their world. It is 1855. Cars and airplanes have not yet been invented. Trains are a novelty for those traveling to cities—and even people using the newly built railroads still rely on horses to get to and from the station.

In towns and rural areas throughout Europe and the Americas, horses are the most important type of transportation. They carry riders on their backs and haul passengers and cargo. Horse-drawn wagons transport goods from factories and farms; horse-drawn carriages take people from place to place.

Buying and selling horses is a serious business. It is the reason that many of the people in John Herring's painting have come to Barnet Fair. For hundreds of years, gatherings such as this one have taken place on set dates all over Great Britain. Barnet Fair is one of the most famous in the country. It has taken place twice each year since 1588. Its main purpose is to bring together buyers and sellers of livestock—cattle, ponies, and horses.

In the mid-1800s, when this picture was painted, about 10,000 people attended the fair every day. Some came to inspect the 40,000 animals for sale, others to enjoy horse races, boxing matches, and stalls selling refreshments and souvenirs. People came from near and far. Londoners enjoyed a short day trip, while farmers from the remotest corners of Great Britain needed several days to make the journey and to try to make the best deals. These visitors depended mostly on horses to get to the fair (only those who lived nearby could walk).

The fair still takes place today, but amusements and rides have become the main attraction. In 2005, only 20 horses were sold at Barnet Fair.

BARNET FAIR, 1855, JOHN FREDERICK HERRING, SR.

Fair purchase *The man leading this string of horses might be a dealer showing off his stock, or a satisfied customer heading home with his new purchases. Because Barnet Fair was only a few miles north of London, it was a convenient place for the drivers of the city's horse-drawn cabs to purchase new animals.*

Rear guard *The man riding at the back of the coach, wearing the same style of red vest as the driver up front, is the guard. Like the conductor on a train or the cabin crew on a plane, he is responsible for his passengers' safety. Some guards carried weapons to protect their coaches from highway robbers.*

Blind leading the blind *This carriage horse wears a bridle with leather blinders, attached next to each of its eyes, to limit how much the horse can see. These devices have been used for at least 2,500 years to prevent horses from being distracted or alarmed by passing traffic. Frightened horses may rear up so suddenly that passengers are flung out of the carriage.*

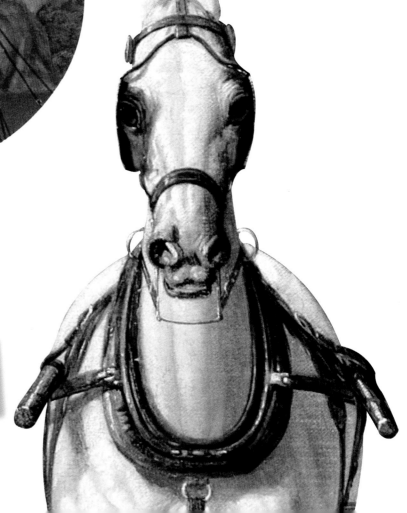

JOHN FREDERICK HERRING, SR.
1795–1865
The English painter John Frederick Herring, Sr. specialized in creating pictures of horses, hunting, sporting scenes, and other images of country life. His work was popular among wealthy British noblemen and the owners of large country estates. His artistic talent must have run in the family, because his three sons and his brother were also successful painters.

OUT FOR A RIDE

FOR THOUSANDS OF YEARS, HUMANS HAVE RELIED ON THE HORSE for transportation. Horses can move quickly, faster than people can walk. They are strong enough to carry people or baggage on their backs, or to pull a heavy load. Unlike many other animals, they can also be taught to obey a rider's commands.

In this painting by the French artist Pierre Auguste Renoir, the two people are enjoying a leisurely ride in the outskirts of Paris. The lady and her young companion, who might be either her son or her little brother, come from a wealthy family. They are wearing fashionable clothes designed especially for riding. The animals have glossy coats, which suggests they are well cared for and well fed. Both riders look relaxed and confident. They probably learned to ride at an early age, almost as soon as they could sit on a horse. Wealthy families hired private riding teachers for their children.

At the time Renoir painted this picture, in 1873, only people who had plenty of money and free time rode horses just for fun. Their horses were lucky, too. Most horses spent their lives working hard as beasts of burden or members of the military. By carrying soldiers into battle, they faced the same dangers as the men who rode them.

Getting into the habit
This stylish black top hat, designed to look like those worn by city gentlemen of the day, is an essential part of any fashion-conscious, nineteenth-century horsewoman's riding outfit, or habit. The gauze veil was designed to protect the wearer from dust and grit stirred up by the horse's hooves.

Lucky horseshoes
The practice of protecting horses' hooves with flat metal shoes goes back at least 1,000 years. Blacksmiths make and attach the shoes, which need to be replaced frequently. The blacksmith's workshop is as necessary to these horse owners as the gas station will be to car owners in centuries to come.

PIERRE AUGUSTE RENOIR
1841–1919
Pierre Auguste Renoir was a famous French painter and a friend of many other great artists, including Monet, Cézanne, and Degas. He was a leader in the art movement known as Impressionism. Impressionists use lively colors and quick brushstrokes to capture the world around them. In the 1870s, Renoir became famous for detailed portraits, such as this one showing elegant Parisians at home or at play.

Putting his foot in it
Stirrups were probably first used in northern China. They appeared in Europe about the sixth century A.D. Stirrups help a rider stay in the saddle and make the horse easier to mount. Before stirrups, riders vaulted onto the animal's back or climbed onto a mounting block to be hoisted onto the saddle.

HORSEWOMAN IN THE BOIS DE BOULOGNE, 1873, PIERRE AUGUSTE RENOIR

THE RAILROAD STATION

I T IS 1875, AND THE RAILROAD STATION in Vienna, the capital of Austria, is bustling. The station is crowded with passengers arriving or departing, friends who have come to greet or see off the travelers. There are also many people working on the railroad—the engineer, a mechanic, conductors, porters, and a paperboy. The building itself is like a great cathedral built of stone, glass, and cast iron, dedicated to the mighty steam engine, or locomotive, and the iron rails that allow it to pull freight and passengers across the land at speeds people had never known before.

As early as the 1700s, British inventors had begun to experiment with machinery that could use the power of steam. In 1804, a pioneering locomotive built by Richard Trevithick showed just what a steam-driven engine could do—it pulled a line of rail cars carrying 70 men and 10 tons (9 tonnes) of iron for 9 miles (14.5 km) in just 2 hours. This would have taken several teams of workhorses all day.

The first railroad in North America, the Baltimore and Ohio Railroad, began running in 1827. By 1830, travelers could ride on the first American-built passenger train. Over the next 30 years, businessmen spent—and made—huge amounts of money building railroads to carry both passengers and freight, especially in the northeastern United States, where most of the country's factories were located.

During the Civil War, this railroad network helped the industrialized North gain an advantage over the less-developed Confederate states. Railroads carrying supplies from northern factories to the combat zone became a key part of the Union Army's war strategy. Military engineers maintained existing lines, built and repaired bridges, and constructed new sections of track. Once the Confederacy surrendered, railroad-building played an important part in rebuilding the South. After the Civil War, growth in railroads surged. By 1869, the tracks ran from coast to coast.

CARL KARGER
1848–1913

Carl Karger lived in Vienna and flourished as an artist when the Austrian capital was at the peak of its prosperity. As a teenager in 1864, he began to study at the Vienna Academy of Fine Arts. During his long working life, Karger created frescoes, ceiling paintings, and other lavish interior decorations for the Vienna State Opera House, the Burgtheater, and other magnificent new public buildings in the city.

NORTHWEST TRAIN STATION, VIENNA, 1875
CARL KARGER

Carrying the load

A porter in a leather apron is hoping these passengers will pay him to carry their bags. The railroads created thousands of new jobs, ranging from skilled and well-paid engineers (drivers) and station managers to the humble laborers who swept the platforms.

Bright idea

The headlights on the front of this locomotive are oil lamps, probably burning coal-based kerosene. They make it possible for trains to run at night, allowing railroad companies to offer nighttime departures and long-distance journeys that did not have to be limited to daylight hours.

All steamed up *The locomotive's boiler heats up water to create the steam that keeps the engine running. It burns huge amounts of coal, which has given the mining industry a great boost. Not only are the railroads the biggest buyers of coal, they also transport the fuel quickly and cheaply to distant markets.*

Better safe than sorry *This "wheel tapper" is checking the wheels to make sure they are balanced. If they aren't, the train might jump off the rails. Terrible accidents in the early years of rail travel led to the invention of several safety devices. Air brakes, developed by George Westinghouse in 1868, helped trains to stop more quickly in an emergency.*

Greeting the arrivals *The boy in the straw hat and the stylish adults with him have come to the station to meet someone arriving in Vienna by train. Rail travel changed society by making it easier to stay in touch with friends, family, and business contacts far away. In the mid-1800s, an Englishman wrote that thanks to the train, young people looking for someone to marry no longer had to limit their choices to those living in the same town.*

SEEING THE SIGHTS

THE EXCITED PASSENGERS IN THIS PAINTING by the nineteenth-century German artist Adolph von Menzel show one of the many ways that railroads changed the lives of people living in industrialized countries. Menzel named his picture "On a Journey to Beautiful Countryside." The people he painted are clearly happy to be doing something that would have been unthinkable just a few years ago. They are traveling somewhere just for the fun of it.

Before the arrival of the steam locomotive, journeys of any distance were uncomfortable, slow, and often dangerous. Most people thought of mountains, deserts, and other wild areas as frightening rather than beautiful. However, between the 1840s and the 1890s, thousands of workers toiled all over the United States and Europe, laying down tracks across the wilderness, blasting tunnels through mountainsides, and building bridges across wide rivers and deep gorges.

Thanks to the efforts made by these workers, it became possible to move smoothly and quickly across the land by rail. Americans and Europeans alike discovered the joys of sightseeing. Anyone who could afford a train ticket and had a little time to spare could become a tourist. Travel companies sprang up to take people on short day trips, guided tours, and long vacations. Hotels and restaurants prospered in scenic spots. So did stores selling souvenirs. A whole new industry was born.

ADOLPH VON MENZEL
1815–1905
Adolph Friedrich Erdmann von Menzel was born in Breslau, Germany (now Wroclaw, Poland). At the age of 14 he began work as a lithographer (a type of printmaker) at the printing press run by his father. He established himself as one of Germany's leading illustrators, where he is admired for his accurately observed and detailed images of historic subjects, as well as for his scenes taken from daily life.

ON A JOURNEY TO BEAUTIFUL COUNTRYSIDE, 1892, ADOLPH FRIEDRICH ERDMANN VON MENZEL

Spectacular views *The man holding the binoculars looks as though he is seeing something amazing through the window of the train. By the 1850s and 1860s, European rail passengers could take advantage of organized sightseeing trips to scenic destinations, such as the Swiss Alps, the Scottish Highlands, or the Rhine River Valley.*

Traveling in style *The lady's red dress, beaded jacket, and flowery hat show off her sense of fashion. The clothes—and the bouquet she carries— show how conditions had improved for nineteenth-century rail travelers since the early days of steam. At first, passengers rode in open, windowless cars, and their clothing was blackened by smoke from the locomotive.*

Doing it by the book *This red book—popular among tourists—is one of a series of travel guides produced by the German publisher Karl Baedeker in the mid-1800s. He realized that the growth of rail travel created a market for books giving information about a country's scenery, history, sights, and hotels.*

Tickets please! *The conductor is responsible for checking that passengers have paid their fares and for looking after them on the train. He wears a military-style uniform that gives him an air of authority when inspecting tickets or demanding payment. It is also designed to show that he—like soldiers in an army—belongs to a large and well-disciplined organization.*

You get what you pay for *The well-upholstered seat, with its polished wooden armrests, shows that this is the part of the train reserved for passengers who have paid a higher fare. European trains are traditionally divided into different classes. A first-class ticket buys a comfortable seat in a compartment with plenty of room to move around. In other, cheaper sections of the train, people are packed into tighter spaces, with harder seats and less room for their belongings.*

Rock-a-bye baby *Exhausted by all the excitement of the outing, or simply lulled by the movement of the train, this young tourist has fallen blissfully asleep. The earliest trains rattled and jolted along the track. However, by the time this picture was painted in 1892, improvements to rails and track beds meant that travelers enjoyed a much smoother ride.*

TRAFFIC JAM

GRIDLOCK IS NOTHING NEW. URBAN STREETS HAVE BEEN JAMMED with different kinds of traffic for thousands of years. The invention of motorized vehicles have just made it worse. This bustling scene of Ludgate Hill, in London, England, was painted by Christiaan Pieter Snijders at the beginning of the twentieth century. It shows a moment in history when old and new forms of transportation exist side by side. Double-decker buses powered by engines share the streets with horse-drawn wagons, people with wheelbarrows or carts, pedestrians, and cyclists.

At the time when motor vehicles first appeared on the scene, there were around 30 million horses in the United States, and 3.5 million in Great Britain. One horse was estimated to produce around 45 pounds (20 kg) of manure every day. Many people welcomed the arrival of the "horseless carriage" on the grounds that it left the streets much cleaner. City dwellers, who always seemed to be in a hurry, liked the fact that a motor vehicle could reach speeds of 20 or 30 miles (30 or 50 km) per hour. This was at least five times faster than the average horse-drawn vehicle. However, country folk complained that these new speed machines were a danger to their livestock, their pets, and all wild creatures. On one road trip through Iowa in the early 1900s, a state official counted about 225 dead animals from 29 wild and domestic species.

Taxi! Taxi! *Starting in the late 1500s, horse-drawn carriages were a common way to travel around London. Four-wheeled models, such as the vehicle pictured here—known as a "growler"—first appeared in the 1830s and could be seen on the streets until the 1930s, long after the arrival of the automobile.*

Long arm of the law *Police officers have always controlled drivers' speed and behavior. In the 1890s, British policemen used stopwatches to make sure motorists did not travel faster than 4 miles (6 km) per hour—the speed of a horse-drawn carriage.*

CHRISTIAAN PIETER SNIJDERS
1881–1943
Christiaan Snijders was born in the seaport city of Rotterdam in the Netherlands. He was a self-taught artist and printmaker. In spite of his lack of formal training, he was a keen social observer. Visiting London in the early 1900s, he captured details of the city's crowded streets that are almost like photographs in their ability to preserve a moment in time.

LUDGATE HILL (DETAIL), *c.* 1910–20, CHRISTIAAN PIETER SNIJDERS

Hitch your wagon *The unseen horse hitched to this cart is one of 50,000 horses that pulled vehicles in London at any given time in the 1900s. Breweries, coal merchants, and metal dealers used specially bred workhorses to haul wagons full of goods around American and British cities.*

Wheels of fortune *By pedaling through the city, this cyclist is taking part in a transportation revolution. By the 1900s, cheap, mass-produced bicycles enabled workers to travel farther from home than ever before, increasing their job opportunities.*

A necessary evil? *This ornate iron railroad bridge provided an important link in London's transportation network. It allowed a line that carried freight and passengers from docks at Dover to connect to rail services running through the city. However, many people complained that it spoiled a famous view of St. Paul's Cathedral (the dome and tower seen at the back—see above).*

Welcome aboard *The term* bus *comes from* omnibus, *a Latin word that means "for all." The first public omnibus service, using horse-drawn vehicles that carried up to 18 passengers, began in Paris in 1819. In the early twentieth century, horsepower gave way to engine power on both sides of the Atlantic Ocean. London's first motor bus appeared in 1897; New York's first motor bus arrived in 1905.*

In a jam *The laborer pushing an old-fashioned handcart may reach his destination faster than the new motor bus idling nearby. Cities struggled to control the ever-growing number and variety of vehicles crowding their streets. Traffic jams and fatal crashes were a normal daily occurrence. Automatic traffic signals did not arrive in the United States until 1914 or in Great Britain until 1927.*

A word from our sponsor *Advertisements such as those on these crowded double-decker buses have been a familiar sight on public transportation since the days of the horse-drawn omnibus. Bovril, the product being promoted on the front of the first bus, is a beef-flavored hot drink first marketed in 1886 and still sold in Great Britain today.*

A NIGHT ON THE TOWN

IT IS 1928, AND NEW YORK CITY is the biggest metropolis in the United States. It is the center of many powerful businesses, and a place where people are always on the move—thanks to a growing rapid transit system. John Sloan's painting of this busy corner in the Greenwich Village neighborhood in Manhattan brings to life the energy and excitement of the city just after nightfall. The working day is over. Some New Yorkers are heading home, while others are out for an evening's entertainment.

Overhead, elevated trains thunder by on raised tracks. The first elevated train service began in Manhattan in 1870, and the network expanded over the next three decades. By the time this picture was painted, elevated trains were carrying 384 million passengers each year. Underground, subway trains roar through tunnels at 40 miles (65 km) per hour, shrinking distances even further. At street level, pedestrians compete for space with electrically powered trolley cars, motor buses, trucks, and the popular automobile.

The same thing is happening in other large American and European cities, such as Boston, Chicago, London, and Paris. Even those living miles out of town can now travel easily into the center, where most of the jobs are. By giving many more people access to a wider range of economic, educational, and social opportunities, increasingly fast and efficient public transportation systems are helping cities to prosper as never before.

JOHN SLOAN
1871–1951

John Sloan began his career as an illustrator for the *Philadelphia Inquirer* newspaper in 1892. In 1902, he moved to Greenwich Village in New York City, home to many artists and writers. Many of his paintings documented the lives and neighborhoods of New York's poorest people. With several other painters interested in the realities of city life, he founded an artistic movement known as the "Ashcan School."

THE SIXTH AVENUE ELEVATED AT THIRD STREET, 1928, JOHN SLOAN

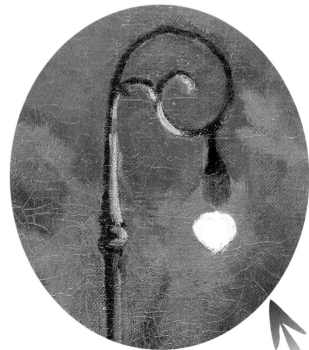

City lights *Electric lights allow New Yorkers to move freely around the city even after dark. Offices and businesses can stay open later. And once working hours are over, stores, restaurants, and theaters welcome customers with a blaze of light. Although New York City switched from dim gas bulbs to electric streetlights in the mid-1880s, the first American community to switch on the streetlights was tiny Attalla, Alabama, in 1882.*

The El *The New York "El" train runs on tracks ranging from 20 to 63 feet (6 to 19 m) above street level. People living in second- and third-floor apartments have to live with the deafening clatter of trains passing close to their windows every few minutes—day and night—until the last elevated line is closed in 1955.*

An accident waiting to happen *The young woman on the right looks worried as her two friends dash recklessly in front of an oncoming car. As cars become more common, so do traffic accidents. Neither drivers nor pedestrians realize how much damage an automobile can do to a person. In 1924, four years before Sloan painted this picture, over 23,000 Americans died in road accidents, and 700,000 were injured.*

Out and about *These young women, ready for a night on the town, have much more freedom than their mothers did. In the 1920s, attitudes about female employment are changing. In cities, a whole range of new jobs have opened up for women looking for work outside the home. Public transportation makes it possible for them to take advantage of these opportunities.*

On the right track *The bridge that the El runs on is just wide enough for two sets of tracks, and the trains will come dangerously close as they pass each other. Signal boxes, such as this one, warned train drivers they were approaching potentially dangerous points, such as where tracks turned a corner or branched off from the main line.*

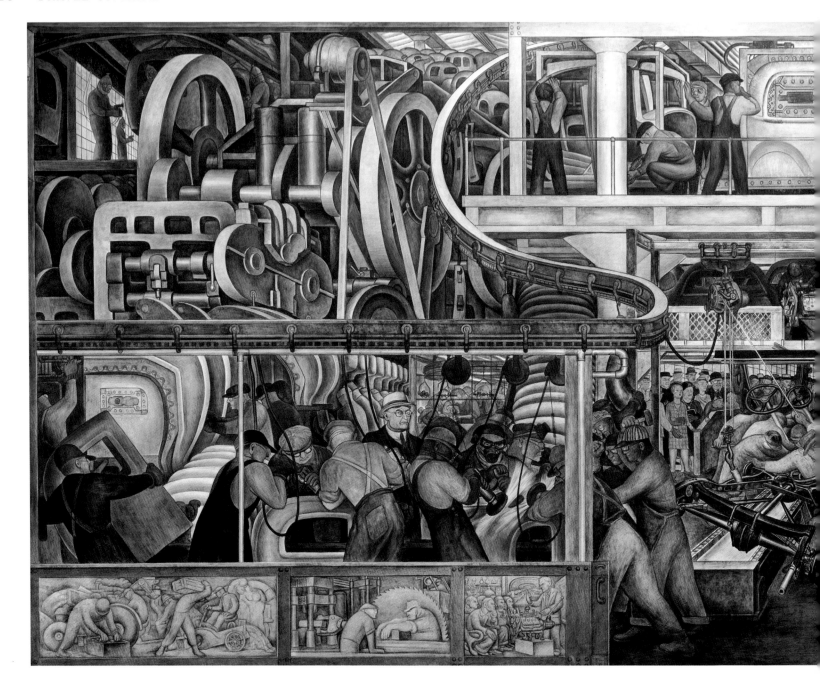

Getting Behind the Wheel

I is the early 1900s, and automobiles are so expensive to buy and to run that only wealthy people can afford them. These cars are hard to handle and often break down. However, a pioneering manufacturer named Henry Ford is about to change everything. In 1908, he introduces a new type of car that is inexpensive enough for ordinary workers to buy, easy to drive, and reliable. Ford has decided to call it the Model T.

Customers snapped up Ford's new automobile as fast as his factory in Detroit could make them. In 1900, there had been fewer than 8,000 cars registered in the United States. By 1910, two years after the Model T came onto the market, there were about 500,000 cars. By 1924, two-thirds of all registered cars on American roads were Fords.

The materials used to make the car's chassis (the body of the car) and improvements to the engine and

THE DETROIT INDUSTRY MURALS (DETAIL), 1932–33, DIEGO RIVERA

the electrical wiring helped to keep the price low. However, the real secret of Ford's success was the system he pioneered for building his vehicles. He was the first manufacturer to use assembly lines, in which each worker had a specific task, so parts could be put together quickly. His factory at River Rouge, near Detroit—depicted here by the Mexican mural-painter Diego Rivera—turned out 1,000 cars each day. The twentieth century was truly the age of the automobile.

DIEGO RIVERA
1886–1957

Diego Rivera, born in Guanajuato, Mexico, believed that art could change the world for the better. In the 1920s, he created huge frescoes for Mexico's public buildings, gaining international fame. In 1931, Rivera was asked to paint a set of murals documenting Detroit's industrial achievements. The resulting artworks are dramatic tributes to the machinery—and the workers—of the automotive age.

A watchful eye *The man in the white hat keeps a close eye on workers bent over a chassis. His name is Mead Bricker, a production manager at the plant for over 20 years. Bricker became famous for speeding up the assembly line by forcing staff to work faster and faster. Anyone unable to stand the pace was fired.*

Stamping press *This massive machine is a stamping press. It dwarfs the workers who tend it as it handles huge sheets of steel, shaping them into fenders and other car-body parts. Fascinated by this enormous device, Diego Rivera sketched it many times. It reminded him of an ancient Mexican god demanding sacrifices from terrified mortals.*

Assembly time *The two men in overalls are spot welders. They are sealing the separate sections of the car together using intense heat and high pressure. They have little room to move around. In Ford's system for speeding up the manufacturing process, machines and work stations for each part of the operation were positioned close together.*

Power struggle *The engine being carried along on a pulley, ready to be lowered into place, will run on gasoline. Early cars had been powered by steam or electricity, but Henry Ford rejected these methods. He insisted that the only way to make a car that most Americans could afford was to install a gasoline engine.*

The new sewing circle *Sitting at a table, women sew upholstery for car interiors. Apart from sewing and a few other light assembly tasks, most Ford factory jobs are reserved for men until the start of World War II. When many male employees leave for the army, the company must turn to its female workforce to do the heavier production jobs.*

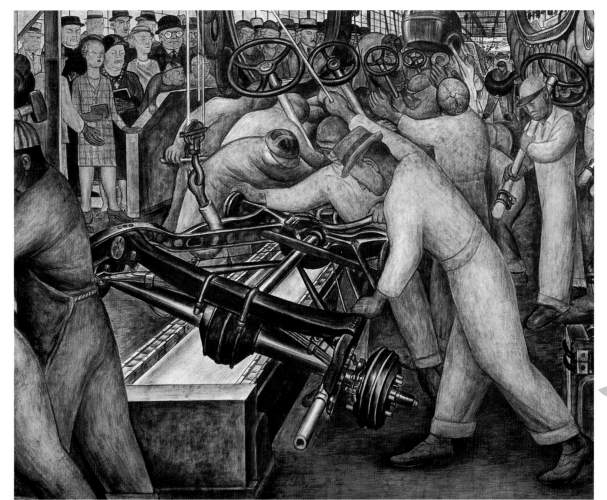

Ready to roll *Another Ford car makes its way along the assembly line as its sections are put together. Ford perfected techniques for producing automobiles in huge quantities, saving time and money at every stage. In 1913, his factory took 12 hours to produce a single Model T. A year later, it could turn out the same car in 1 hour and 33 minutes—and it could make 1,000 cars a day.*

Riding the Waves

HUMANS HAVE ALWAYS FACED THE DANGERS OF TRAVELING BY WATER.
OVER THE CENTURIES, SHIPBUILDERS HAVE LOOKED FOR NEW WAYS
TO CONQUER THE POWER OF THE WAVES AND WINDS.

Picture this! The date is July 3, 1952. You are part of an excited crowd that has gathered on Pier 86, on the waterfront in New York City. Today is the maiden voyage for the largest and most advanced passenger liner ever built in the United States. Because your father works for the shipping company that owns her, you are lucky enough to be there on this historic day to watch the SS *United States* depart on its first transatlantic crossing.

Your head is buzzing with facts and figures: The ship is 990 feet, 6 inches (302 m) long. She is like a floating city, towering above the dock. She is designed to carry up to 2,000 passengers in comfort, along with 1,000 crew members. Within two days' notice, she can also be converted into a military transport ship capable of carrying over 14,000 troops. This is not as strange as it sounds. In World War II, which ended only seven years ago, many passenger liners were adapted to serve the war effort by ferrying soldiers overseas.

Above all, the SS *United States* is built for speed. Thanks to her four engines—generating 268,000 horsepower—she had the potential to reach a speed up to 43 knots (the equivalent of 50 miles or 80 km per hour on land). She can travel 10,000 miles (16,000 km) before she needs to refuel. And, although you won't know this for another few days, she is about to smash the existing speed records for passenger ships, reaching England in an outstanding 3 days, 10 hours, and 40 minutes.

Sea travel has improved a lot since the days when the Pilgrims crossed the Atlantic on the

EUROPEAN SAILORS *were eager to explore places beyond their maps in the Middle Ages. Sturdy wooden vessels, such as these ships in a boatyard in Venice, were built for long ocean voyages.*

THE FIRST STEAMSHIPS had engines that heated water to create a buildup of steam, which turned paddle wheels. These ships came into use in the United States and Europe in the early 1800s. The paddle steamer Syracuse, *shown here, was built in 1857 as a towboat on the Hudson River.*

Mayflower. It took them 66 days to make the crossing, with 102 passengers, 25 to 30 crew members, and a variety of farm animals crammed into a sailing ship about 90 feet (27.5 m) long and 25 feet (7.5 m) wide. Each family had a tiny area of space belowdecks for themselves and all their possessions. Anyone taller than 5 feet (1.5 m) had to crouch to avoid hitting the ceiling.

Generations of European immigrants arrived in North America in conditions not much better than these. However, they were lucky in comparison to people from West Africa who were kidnapped and brought across the Atlantic in slave ships. They were packed in like cargo, lying in rows side by side and chained in place for the whole journey.

You have heard these stories. You come from a long line of seafarers. So you know just

how much life has changed for those men and women who work on or travel the seven seas. Your grandfather, who was born in 1880, began his career as a merchant seaman on a three-masted, square-rigged "down-easter," carrying grain from the East Coast to California. His brother captained one of the last of the paddle-wheel steamers on the Hudson River. Your aunt served as a nurse on a U.S. Navy hospital ship during the war.

When you grow up, you would like to follow the family tradition and do something connected to the sea and ships. Someday you might command a vessel even larger and faster than the SS *United States.* However, you think you will start with something slightly smaller. Tomorrow you are going out into Long Island Sound for a sailing lesson on your cousin's small dinghy.

FERRIES CARRY PEOPLE and their cars for short distances across bays and rivers. The Staten Island Ferry, shown here, began its service to Manhattan in 1817.

VENETIAN VESSELS

THE BUSY HARBOR IN THIS SCENE, by the famous eighteenth-century Italian artist known as Canaletto, is in the heart of the great city of Venice. This Italian city-state was built on a cluster of 118 islands in a shallow lagoon, which are linked by 150 large and small canals. It was no wonder that Venetians developed masterful skills as shipbuilders and sailors.

Between the fourteenth and sixteenth centuries, the Venetians dominated European trade with the Middle East. They saw themselves as Europe's defender against threats from the east, which were posed by another great power trying to command the seas—the Ottoman Empire, ruled from the Turkish capital, Constantinople (now Istanbul). To ensure their mastery of the seas, Venetians built a huge district of shipyards, docks, warehouses, and workshops known as the Arsenale. Within this vast complex, craftsmen turned out state-of-the-art ships equipped for long-distance trade and exploration—or for war.

By the mid-1700s, when Canaletto painted this picture, Venice's glory days were over. However, its seafarers, and others throughout Europe, were enjoying the benefits of new technology. Vessels could travel farther than ever before, exploring all the world's oceans. New navigational aids, such as the sextant and the chronometer, meant that, no matter how far a ship might sail, it could find its way home again.

Even with all these changes, smaller seagoing merchant ships, such as the wooden vessel in this picture, were still similar in shape and materials to those used in ancient Rome 1,500 years earlier. Such vessels continue to have a round hull, or body, and square rigging.

CANALETTO
1697–1768
Canaletto, whose real name was Giovanni Antonio Canale, was born in Venice. He was one of the first artists to become famous for painting city views. His atmospheric images of Venetian canals and festivals sold well to wealthy English visitors, who brought them home as souvenirs. From 1746 to 1755 he worked in England, painting landscapes and architectural views.

THE RIVA DEGLI SCHIAVONI, 1736
CANALETTO

Luxury lodgings *The rows of large windows high in the stern of this ship provide light for the largest and most comfortable living spaces—the captain's cabin, the officers' quarters, and compartments for important passengers on board. However, most compartments on eighteenth-century vessels were dark, cramped, and airless. Ordinary crew members slept belowdecks in canvas hammocks with little space between them.*

Venice's trademark *Since the eleventh century, the wooden gondola has transported passengers through Venice. It is thin enough to navigate the narrowest of the city's canals. The little shelter on deck was standard on gondolas at the time Canaletto painted this scene. Early gondolas were decorated with gilt—a thin layer of gold—but a government ruling in 1562 allowed only black paint to be used on the boats.*

Merchants of Venice *It would not be surprising to find that the Venetians deep in conversation by the canal are talking business. Their three-cornered hats and long cloaks suggest that they are prosperous merchants. The nearby buildings include a warehouse for holding cargo and a bakery that produces ship's biscuits—the staple food of long-distance seafarers. They were hard, dry, and not very delicious, but they could last for a long time at sea without going stale.*

Waterway workhorse *This sturdy wooden boat is used for transporting local freight, such as fresh produce for the city's markets, or for fishing in the lagoon. Because it is symmetrical—with both ends of the same shape and size—either end of the craft can be used as the bow or the stern. This flexibility makes it ideal for use in canals where there is no space for a boat to turn around.*

In pole position *Venetians developed special skills to steer their small craft through the city's cramped canals, which were crisscrossed by 400 humpbacked bridges. To make sure they could see any obstacles ahead, boatmen stood up, propelling the boat with a long pole instead of oars. Because the water was so shallow, boats were built with flat bottoms instead of V-shaped bottoms.*

HEADING FOR DISASTER

O N THIS SUMMER'S DAY IN 1838, the seagoing paddle steamer SS *Forfarshire* leaves the docks at Hull, England, bound for the port of Dundee in Scotland. She is carrying 63 passengers and crew, along with a cargo of cloth, soap, and other goods. Local artist John Ward's painting of her departure may look like the illustration of an ordinary day at a busy English harbor, but it is a picture of an accident about to happen. It shows that even on a normal day, seafaring can be a dangerous business.

As the newly built *Forfarshire* heads up along the English coast, passing the rocky Farne Islands, her boiler springs a leak. Scalding water bursts out, stopping the engines and filling the engine room with steam. To make matters worse, a storm closes in. Unable to reach the engine to repair it, the crew hoists the ship's sails and tries to move the stricken vessel to more sheltered waters. Unfortunately, the heaving seas throw the steamer straight onto the rocks, tearing it in two before most passengers could reach the lifeboats.

Only nine of those on board make their way onto a larger rock. They would have died if it had not been for the daring actions of a local lighthouse keeper and his 22-year-old daughter, Grace Darling, who rowed through the storm and risked their own lives to bring the survivors safely ashore.

JOHN WARD
1798–1849

John Ward was born in the seaport of Hull, on the northeast coast of England. He began his career as a painter and decorator, working on houses, ships, and store signs in this busy harbor town. By his late 30s, he had become an artist with a special interest in maritime, or ocean, scenes. His paintings were widely admired for their clear and accurate depiction of naval details.

SS FORFARSHIRE *LEAVING HULL ON HER LAST VOYAGE, c.* 1838–40
JOHN WARD

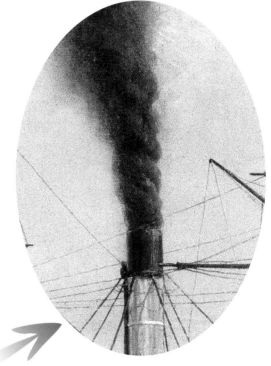

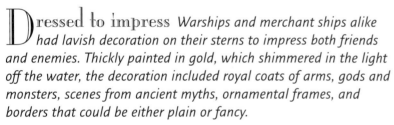

Dressed to impress *Warships and merchant ships alike had lavish decoration on their sterns to impress both friends and enemies. Thickly painted in gold, which shimmered in the light off the water, the decoration included royal coats of arms, gods and monsters, scenes from ancient myths, ornamental frames, and borders that could be either plain or fancy.*

Something in the air *At first glance, there seems nothing out of the ordinary about the smoke rising from the Forfarshire's stack. Its engines are working up a full head of steam as the paddle steamer gets underway. However, Ward created this painting after the shipwreck, so the black plume serves as an eerie warning of disaster to come.*

Sidekick *The Forfarshire's paddle wheels are on the side of the ship. On some steamboats, the wheels were located at the rear. Paddle steamers were first used on rivers and were making sea journeys by the 1820s. They were popular in Europe for short passenger routes, between Mediterranean ports, and around the British Isles.*

A long haul *Dangling from a wooden beam jutting out from the deck, a system of ropes, hooks, and pulleys stands ready to lift or lower cargo or supplies. Loading and unloading was a slow process. Everything had to be transferred between the ship and much smaller boats, known as tenders, which served as ferries between the large ships and the shore.*

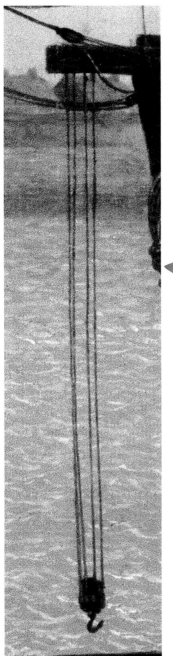

The red duster *The flag flying from this three-masted sailing ship identifies it as a British merchant vessel. Known as the red ensign, or the red duster, the flag's upper left-hand corner bears Great Britain's national emblem— the Union Jack. At the time Ward painted this picture, Britain had the best ships and did the most trading with overseas nations.*

Barging in *These three men look relaxed as they survey the harbor while standing and sitting on a wooden float, which consists of a stack of timber poles and logs lashed together. The float is connected by a towrope to a barge. These shallow, flat-bottomed vessels were used to transport freight along inland waterways.*

SAILING INTO THE SUNSET

WHEN THE PAINTER JAMES JACQUES TISSOT ASKED A FRIEND to pose with his family for this scene aboard a ship called "The Last Evening," he created a mystery. Did Tissot intend the painting to show a ship's first mate's last evening with his sweetheart before the ship sails away? Or is the lady a passenger the officer has fallen in love with on a voyage that has just ended?

Tissot may have deliberately kept the details of the love story a mystery, but the information he has given us about the ship and its surroundings tell another story, of passenger travel in the 1870s. By this time, regular steamship services are carrying passengers and cargo across the Atlantic. They also make the long voyage around South America—the only sea route between the east and west coasts of the United States. Although steamships are now popular, new sailing ships are being designed to compete with them. The masts and rigging tell us that this sailing ship is possibly one of the new generation of fast vessels known as clippers.

The rows of white lifeboats on deck show that safety is now taken seriously. In the 1850s, governments had begun to pass laws regulating safety at sea. However, the well-polished woodwork and wicker chairs indicate that the shipping line wants its passengers to enjoy, rather than simply survive, their journey.

JAMES JACQUES TISSOT
1836–1902

The French artist Jacques Tissot began his career as a painter of historical scenes, but he soon began to specialize in pictures of modern life. He moved to London in 1871 and became famous for "conversation pieces," paintings that hinted at an untold story. He fell in love with Kathleen Newton, an Englishwoman, and used her—along with other friends—as models for these scenes.

THE LAST EVENING, 1873
JAMES JACQUES TISSOT

Afloating forest *As we can see from the maze of masts and rigging behind it, this ship is berthed alongside other sailing vessels. Until the 1850s, most sails had been rigged with ropes made of hemp—the best of it from Russia. However, the Crimean War between Great Britain and Russia disrupted hemp supplies, so ships have been using wire rigging instead.*

Master and commander *Because he is seated comfortably on the bridge alongside the captain, the man in the top hat is probably the ship's owner, not an ordinary passenger. The newspaper in the captain's hand may be the English publication Lloyd's List, which began publishing news of ship movements and cargo in 1734 and still exists today.*

A sense of direction *Protected from the elements by a glass window and a handsome brass case, this compass—known as a binnacle compass—was a seafarer's most important navigational tool. The brass cylinders on either side of the compass are oil burners, allowing the navigator to check the ship's position in the dark. A knowledge of stars was also essential for navigation.*

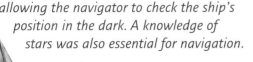

To the lifeboats *By the late 1800s, sea travel was safer than ever before. New ships were stronger and more stable, but the 1912 sinking of the Titanic was a wake-up call. Many of those who died when the liner smashed into an iceberg could have been saved if there had been enough lifeboats on board.*

Boys in blue *The first mate wears a uniform similar to that worn by naval officers, but the logo on his cap is that of the shipping company that employs him. Behind him, the captain wears the same cap. In 1857, the British Navy had introduced jackets with brass buttons as uniforms for chief petty officers. Large commercial shipping companies quickly copied the style.*

Little luxuries *Once shipping companies began competing for passengers, it made good business sense to keep travelers happy during the voyage. The young lady's rocking chair and cozy, warm blanket would have been welcome comforts on a rough crossing. In the 1840s, ships of the pioneering British Cunard line kept a cow on board to supply fresh milk in the middle of the Atlantic.*

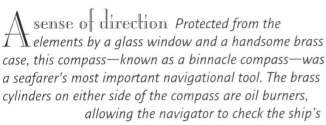

A Day on the Water

T HE MAN AND THREE BOYS IN THIS LATE NINETEENTH-CENTURY PAINTING by American artist Winslow Homer are clearly enjoying their day out on the water. They have been fishing, but it now looks as if they are heading for home.

From an early age, young people—especially boys—growing up in coastal communities usually learn how to handle boats. Some boys are even being prepared to work alongside their fathers as sailors or fishermen. For others, especially those living in remote areas, boats were a common way to get around.

Over the centuries it was generally only the rich who had the time—and the money—to go sailing for pleasure. However, things had changed by the time Winslow Homer painted this picture. For the first time in history, many working people now had weekends free and took vacations. Better wages meant that many Americans living near water could own, or have easy access to, a sailboat. By the late 1800s, recreational sailing clubs had sprung up all over New England and along other coastal areas. Some amateur sailors competed in races. Others, like the four sailors pictured here, were happy just to ride on the currents and daydream as the wind filled their sails.

WINSLOW HOMER
1836–1910
Bostonian Winslow Homer was one of the most important American painters of the nineteenth century. His first major work was inspired by visits to combat areas during the Civil War. In the 1870s, he turned to gentler scenes of country life. In the 1880s, after spending time in an English fishing village, he concentrated on seascapes and dramatic images of humans struggling against nature.

BREEZING UP (A FAIR WIND), 1876
WINSLOW HOMER

Anchors aweigh! *This sailboat's anchor is a traditional design known as a fisherman's anchor. It has two flukes sharp enough to dig down into the seabed and is used in shallow bays and on rocky beaches typical of the Massachusetts coast, where this picture was painted.*

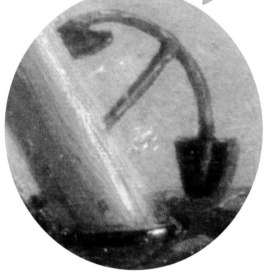

Easy does it *The boy stretching across the bow seems lost in a daydream. Freshly caught fish are just visible inside the boat below him.*

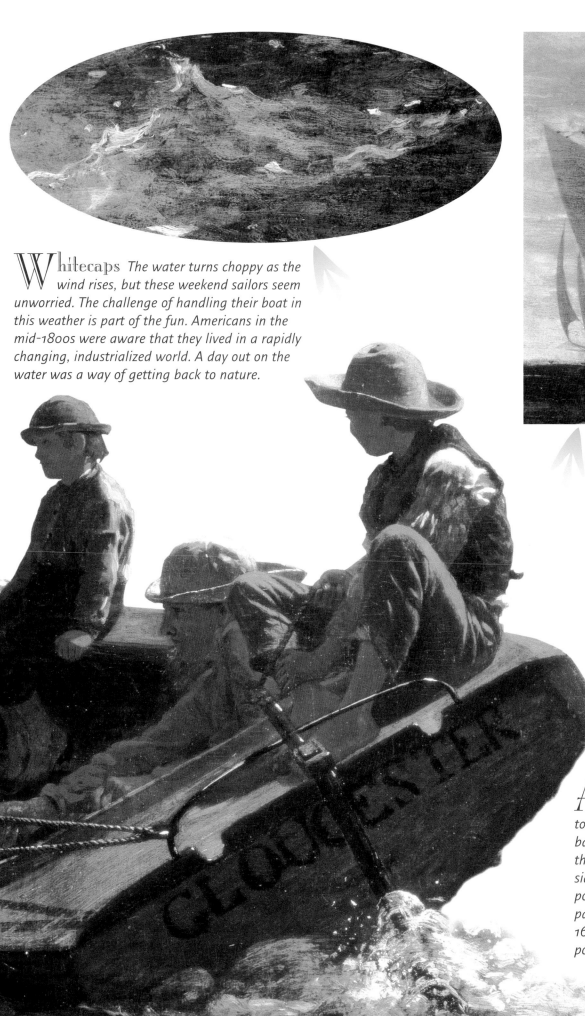

Whitecaps *The water turns choppy as the wind rises, but these weekend sailors seem unworried. The challenge of handling their boat in this weather is part of the fun. Americans in the mid-1800s were aware that they lived in a rapidly changing, industrialized world. A day out on the water was a way of getting back to nature.*

Sails for sale *The larger vessel farther out in the bay might be either another pleasure craft or a working boat used by fishermen. In most coastal communities, specialized trades such as sail making and ship repair played an important part in the local economy, serving the needs of professional seafarers as well as a growing number of amateur boat owners.*

A firm hand on the tiller *The boy uses a length of rope to control the tiller, the horizontal bar attached to the rudder. He steers the vessel by moving it from side to side. The name of the boat's home port, Gloucester, Massachusetts, is painted on the stern. Founded in the 1620s, the town is the oldest fishing port in the United States.*

VICTORY AT SEA

With guns blazing and flags flying, this parade of U.S. Navy ships and civilian vessels makes a grand entrance into New York Harbor. The celebration marks a crucial victory in the Spanish-American War, a war being fought between Spain and the United States in 1898. The cruisers and battleships have just returned from a fight against the Spanish fleet at Santiago de Cuba, in the Caribbean Sea.

The first Navy ship in the line is the USS *New York*. She is an armored cruiser, smaller but faster than a standard battleship and capable of cutting through the seas at a speed of 21 knots. The vessel just behind her, with its two smokestacks rising high, is the battleship *Iowa*. She is one of the newest vessels in the fleet, and she represents the latest in modern warship design. Unlike the *New York*, it is equipped with huge guns that fire powerful explosives and are capable of enormous destruction. The only defense against this degree of firepower is a strong coat of armor. All the ships of the day are built of iron. But the *Iowa*, and other battleships of her class, are also coated with a skin of hardened steel 15 inches (38 cm) thick. Alongside these floating war machines, the ferries, fireboats, tugs, and private yachts make a colorful show—but they look like toys.

FRED PANSING
1854–1912
The German-born artist Fred Pansing spent five years as a sailor before settling in Hoboken, New Jersey, where he concentrated on painting portraits and maritime scenes. Pansing created colorful images of ships in the Cunard and White Star shipping lines, which took center stage on advertising posters, postcards, and even souvenir jigsaw puzzles that were used to promote the ships.

All flags flying *The owners of this yacht are taking part in an old maritime tradition by "dressing the ship" with colorful flags to mark the occasion. Called signal flags, their colors and patterns are part of an internationally recognized maritime code. Long before radios or telephones were invented, such flags were hoisted up to send messages from ship to ship.*

LEADING THE FLEET INTO NEW YORK HARBOR, 1898
FRED PANSING

Ready, aim, fire! *The* New York's *arsenal includes six 8-inch (20-cm) guns, twelve 4-inch (10-cm) guns, and some smaller weapons. Behind her, the battleship* Iowa *is far more heavily armed. On this friendly, festive occasion any firing from the vessels' gun turrets will be done with blank ammunition.*

Standing at attention *The captain of the USS* New York *is almost certainly one of the officers standing on the bridge. His official report on the Battle of Santiago records that "the officers and crew acted in the most enthusiastic and commendable manner. They have worked into so complete a system that the ship is practically instantaneously ready for action."*

ABOVE THE CLOUDS

IN THE TWENTIETH CENTURY, THROUGH THE EFFORTS OF BRAVE
PIONEERS AND DETERMINED INVENTORS, PEOPLE FINALLY FOUND
THEIR WINGS AND TOOK TO THE SKIES.

PICTURE THIS! THE TIME IS NOW. You are sitting in a passenger jet, about to fly from your home in California to visit your grandparents in Florida. You have made this trip often, and the inside of an airplane is almost as familiar as a car. As you wait for takeoff, you think about how air travel began.

An ancient Greek myth tells the story of an inventor called Daedalus. Imprisoned by a hostile king, Daedalus made two pairs of wings out of wax to carry himself and his son Icarus to freedom. He warned Icarus not to fly too high, or the sun's heat would melt the wax. Amazingly, the wings worked. Icarus was so excited that he forgot his father's words and soared up into the heavens. The wings quickly melted, and Icarus fell into the sea and drowned. The story's message was clear: The sky was off-limits.

This tale did not discourage the Italian artist Leonardo da Vinci from trying to design a flying machine in the late 1400s. Nor did it stop the two French passengers on the first-ever manned flight—in a hot-air balloon floating a few hundred feet over Paris in 1783.

As your plane begins to speed along the runway, you think about how Orville and Wilbur Wright must have felt in 1903 when Orville flew the world's first engine-powered airplane 120 feet (36.5 m) across a field in Kitty Hawk, North Carolina. There were few witnesses. The Wrights did not want to spread the news too soon. After making sure that their machine could fly, they wanted to be sure that they would be the first ones to make money from this invention by patenting the plane's design. This meant that anyone who wanted to manufacture an aircraft like theirs would have to pay them for the right to copy the details.

LEONARDO DA VINCI (1452–1519), painter of the Mona Lisa, *was an inventor. His sketchbooks contained diagrams of flying machines, including helicopters.*

WHEN BICYCLE REPAIRMEN *Orville and Wilbur Wright succeeded in getting the world's first real airplane off the ground in 1903, many newspaper editors refused to print the story because they believed it could not possibly be true. Perched on the wing, Orville piloted the craft on its first flight, lasting 12 seconds.*

The world began to pay attention when the Wright Brothers arrived in France (by boat) to show off their plane at the racetrack at Le Mans. The crowd saw the small machine climb 360 feet (110 m), turn circles in the air, and speed along at 40 miles (65 km) per hour.

The race for the skies was on. In 1909, the *Daily Mail*, a London-based newspaper, offered a huge cash prize to the first aviator to fly across the English Channel. Louis Blériot, a French airman, won the money—and gained more international fame for that bumpy flight than the Wright Brothers received for getting airborne in the first place. In 1912, the British Army set up another contest, asking inventors to come up with the best military aircraft. Inspired by these challenges, pilots all over the world began to risk life and limb to find out how far, how high, and how fast these first flying machines could go.

In 1911, another plane designed by the Wright Brothers made the first journey across the United States. It took 84 days and 70 stops. In 1927, Charles Lindbergh flew his *Spirit of St. Louis* on the first nonstop solo flight across the Atlantic.

Now you feel a surge as the wheels leave the ground and your plane starts to climb. You know that a century's worth of engineering skills and technology are lifting you into the sky, but as you look down from a height that even birds can't reach, it still seems like a miracle.

WOMEN BUILT *many of the airplanes used during World War I. They staffed aircraft and weapons factories when male employees left to fight in the war.*

RIDERS IN THE SKY

WHEN ARTIST FRANÇOIS FLAMENG PAINTED THIS BUSY FRENCH AIRFIELD in 1918, World War I was coming to an end. The pilots in the picture have probably just returned from a military mission in their fragile aircraft. However, once peace arrives on November 11, 1918, these men will not be grounded. Their training and experience have given them confidence not only in themselves, but also in their aircraft. The aviators know that these machines have the potential to fly farther and longer than anyone has ever imagined.

This war has spurred rapid advances in technology. At its start, both sides sent up flying machines to get a bird's-eye view of the combat zone. While the pilot steered, an observer—equipped with a camera—examined the state of the enemy forces on the ground to gain accurate information about their troop movements and weapons.

It wasn't long before these crews—flying close to enemy planes doing the same work—began aiming their army revolvers at each other. In 1915, French pilot Roland Garros attached a machine gun to his plane, along with a propeller with blades reinforced to deflect bullets. After shooting down four German planes, he made a forced landing behind enemy lines. Seizing the aircraft along with its pilot, the Germans studied the details of his plane. Both sides now rushed to design strong, fast fighter planes and to train pilots for airborne combat. Once peace arrives, the aviation industry will benefit from these efforts. Soon airplanes will carry both people and cargo across land and ocean. The age of aviation is about to begin.

THE AIRFIELD, 1918, FRANÇOIS FLAMENG

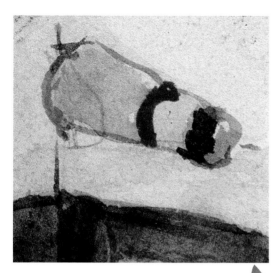

Dressed to chill
Leather helmets with ear flaps, goggles, and warm leather jackets or flying suits with fur collars are essential clothing for these aviators. Early airplanes had open cockpits, exposing pilots to fierce winds and bitter cold. Travelers on the earliest passenger flights had to cram themselves into the cockpit next to the pilot, wearing the same type of protective gear.

Blowing in the wind *A* windsock mounted on a high pole has been a familiar sight at airports since the early days of flight. Pilots landing or taking off can check its position to find out the wind's direction and speed. This windsock is horizontal, standing at a right angle to its pole, showing that the wind is strong. The narrow end points in the direction the wind is blowing.

FRANÇOIS FLAMENG
1856–1923
François Flameng was a painter and a professor at France's Academy of Fine Arts. During World War I, he became one of his country's most valued war artists. His paintings of battle-scarred landscapes and life at the front were widely published. Some of his countrymen criticized his work because it did not glorify war enough to be used as patriotic propaganda.

Spare wheels *These chunky wooden or metal wedges, called chocks, are placed under an aircraft's wheels to make sure that the plane stays still and does not start rolling while it is on the ground. Early aviators used the expression "Chocks away!" to tell the ground crew they were ready for takeoff.*

WINGS OF WAR

THE DEVELOPMENT OF THE AIRPLANE changed the ways that countries could make and fight war, and this first became apparent during World Wars I and II. However, war also made its mark on the development of aviation.

By the time World War II ended in 1945, a huge variety of new aircraft filled the skies. They ranged from enormous transport planes ferrying army units and tanks to tiny helicopters that could land on the roof of a house. Engineering improvements and new materials made all of them stronger, faster, and easier to fly. They were capable of rising higher and staying airborne longer.

However, these achievements came with a price. Once war became airborne, civilians turned into military targets. Bombs of terrible power rained down from unseen enemies above. Some aircraft, such as the Canadian gliders being towed by bombers in this painting by war artist C. C. Turner, had no engines at all. Once hauled into the air and released close to their destination, they depended entirely on their pilots' skill to ride the air currents. Gliders' silent landings made them vital tools in wartime. They could be flown behind enemy lines without being detected.

Inventions that were first developed for military purposes, such as radar navigation and jet engines, would bring peacetime benefits as well. They would make flying easier and safer for future generations, both for the military and for civilian passengers.

GLIDER TRAINING, c. 1944, C. C. TURNER

Tug of war *On this training mission for Canadian glider pilots, a Dakota bomber tows the engineless glider on a rope only 1 inch (2.5 cm) thick. Each glider can carry up to 7,000 pounds (3,175 kg) in weight and are used to ferry troops, nurses, and supplies into combat zones. The planes have no brakes and are easily torn apart by turbulent weather or rough landings.*

Protected from the elements *The crew flying this bomber are lucky to have the protection of an enclosed cockpit. Before World War II, most pilots had to sit in compartments open to the air, exposed to the weather conditions.*

Getting into a spin *From the Wright Brothers' first flight in 1903 until the development of jet engines in the early years of World War II, all planes were driven forward by propellers. These spinning blades, powered by engines attached to the wings, are wing-shaped. Working like a giant fan, they draw the air toward themselves, forcing the plane forward at the same time.*

ARTISTS AT WAR
1914–1945

The artist C. C. Turner was one of many artists recording life at the front during both world wars. Some were ordinary soldiers who sketched what they saw in their diaries. The American, Canadian, and British governments also commissioned official war artists. The director of the U.S. program told his recruits, "Any subject is in order, if as artists you feel that it is part of war."

HIGHWAYS IN THE SKY

THE BUSTLING AIRPORT IN THIS PAINTING may exist only in the artist's imagination, but it looks familiar to anybody who has ever flown. The whole world, or so it seems, is taking off or landing.

It was not always this way. It took many years before the public felt comfortable about flying. After World War I, many former combat pilots earned their living at county fairs, taking thrill seekers up in the air for "joy rides" lasting only a few minutes. In the 1920s, the U.S. government began using airplanes to carry mail across the country. Transporting passengers as well made economic sense, and the aircraft industry began to design planes specifically for the job.

Because flying cost far more than trains or ships, the first passengers were mostly wealthy celebrities or businessmen willing to pay high prices to get somewhere fast. However, conditions were less than luxurious. Planes had no heating and no onboard lavatories. Things were just as primitive on the ground. In its first years, London's Heathrow Airport—today the third busiest in the world—consisted of tents and trailers. By the 1930s, new aircraft designs allowed passengers to fly more comfortably and for longer distances. Some planes were able to land on water and were furnished with sleeping cabins and dining rooms. A ticket on one of these "flying boats" was a luxury that only a few people could afford.

After the end of World War II in 1945, mass passenger travel really did take off. New aircraft designs included wide-bodied jets capable of carrying hundreds of people. Changes in government regulations made flying much more affordable. By the 1960s, airports had to process huge numbers of travelers. Terminals became vast, complicated structures, and passengers spent more time in them than ever before. By 2004, the world's airlines carried some 3.9 billion passengers every year.

JIRO OSUGA
b. 1968

Jiro Osuga was born in Tokyo, Japan, in 1968, and began studying art in England at the age of 18. He attended three of London's most distinguished colleges. His works include witty dramatizations of everyday life, often with himself as the hero of ordinary events turned into incredible adventures. His paintings have been exhibited in Great Britain, the United States, and Hong Kong.

FLIGHT, 1999
JIRO OSUGA

In control The earliest air-traffic control system was a man standing on the field waving signal flags to tell pilots when it was safe to take off. In 1930, aircraft began carrying radios, and the United States' first radio control tower was built in Cleveland, Ohio. Today, air-traffic controllers communicate with pilots by radio to keep aircraft at a safe distance from each other on the ground and in the air.

Under cover An enclosed ramp called a jetway allows passengers to move from the terminal to an airplane without being exposed to the weather or having to climb stairs. Before the jetway's introduction in 1959, people in wheelchairs had to be carried aboard.

Better safe than sorry Walking through a metal detector has been a routine part of air travel since the 1970s, after a series of terrorist hijackings around the world. After 9/11, airport security has become even stricter, with X-rays, bomb-sniffing dogs, and other means of checking both passengers and luggage. The earliest air hijacking on record took place in Peru in 1930.

Wheels on the bus *Other vehicles share the airfield with airplanes. Buses transport passengers at some airports, tow trucks haul cargo, and baggage tractors take luggage from the terminal.*

Stairway to heaven *The first air passengers had to climb a stepladder to board the plane. However, as aircrafts grew larger— with more passengers to board—airports used movable staircases, mounted on wheeled platforms, to help passengers enter and exit the plane. These are still used at some smaller airports.*

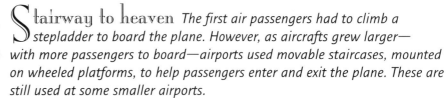

Comings and goings *At the end of the 1920s, the busiest airports handled around 20 flights and 100 passengers daily. Today, Hartsfield Airport in Atlanta, Georgia, tops the global list for arrivals and departures. On a typical day, it sees an average of 2,700 flights, with over 235,000 passengers moving through its terminals.*

Check-in time *In the early days of air travel, airfields and air terminals were smaller. With fewer people flying and no security concerns, check-in was faster, too. Passengers needed only five or ten minutes to get from the front door of the terminal to the plane itself, no matter how much luggage they brought along.*

GLOSSARY

assembly line a series of machines in a factory that are placed in a certain order so they can put an item together as quickly as possible, step by step, from the raw materials to the finished product

aviation the science and technical skills involved in designing, building, and flying aircraft, from simple motor-free gliders to huge jumbo jet planes

aviator a pilot—a person who flies an aircraft

barge a type of flat-bottomed boat that is used to move people and cargo along rivers and canals

battleship the largest of the warships—and the most heavily armed

belowdecks the area inside the hull of a ship, underneath the main deck

bomber an airplane built for dropping bombs

bow the front part of a ship

bridge an area on a ship, or a room, that has the ship's equipment for navigating, or steering, the ship

cargo goods moved from one place to another in a ship or on an airplane, sometimes packed in large containers that can be stacked on top of each other

carriage a wheeled vehicle, pulled by horses, for transporting people

chronometer an instrument for measuring time more accurately than an ordinary watch or clock, used as part

of the navigation equipment on ships and aircraft

clipper a nineteenth-century sailing ship with a sharp bow and large sails, designed to cover long distances quickly and used mainly for cargo

coach a large, enclosed carriage

cockpit the section of an aircraft that holds the pilot, the crew, and the instruments needed to fly a plane

commuter a person who lives in one place and travels to work in another

TIMELINE

1492 Italian inventor Leonardo da Vinci produces diagrams for flying machines. In 1496, he tests one, but it fails

1736 Canaletto paints *The Riva Degli Schiavoni* (pp. 32–35)

c. 1838–40 John Ward paints SS Forfarshire *Leaving Hull on Her Last Voyage* (pp. 36–39)

1873 Pierre Auguste Renoir paints *Horsewoman in the Bois de Boulogne* (pp. 8–9)

1875 Carl Karger paints *Northwest Train Station, Vienna* (pp. 10–13)

1500

1800

1783 The Montgolfier Brothers invent the first hot-air balloons, carrying passengers short distances through the air over Paris

1838 The first two steam-powered ships to cross the Atlantic, the *Sirius* and the *Great Western*, arrive in New York

1855 John Frederick Herring, Sr. paints *Barnet Fair* (pp. 6–7)

1873 James Jacques Tissot paints *The Last Evening* (pp. 40–43)

1868 American inventor George Westinghouse invents compressed air brakes for locomotives, so trains can stop quickly

1876 Winslow Homer paints *Breezing Up (A Fair Wind)* (pp. 44–47)

conductor a person who collects fares on trains

cruiser a warship that is fast, armored, and gunned

elevated train a train that rides on tracks raised above ground level

engineer a person who operates an engine, such as a locomotive

glider an aircraft with wings, but without an engine

hull the body or frame of a boat or ship

industrialized a country or society that has both the skills and the resources to use new technology to make products and increase wealth

locomotive the engine used to pull a train

maritime relating to the sea and to sailing

mast a long pole that rises from the deck of a ship and is used to support the rigging

rigging the ropes and chains used on a ship to raise and lower the sails

rudder the piece of steering equipment attached to the rear of an airplane or the stern of a ship to control its movements

sextant an instrument used by a ship's navigator to measure the distance between the vessel and other objects

stagecoach a carriage that carries both passengers and mail on a regular schedule and at regular stops

steam engine an engine, powered by steam, that drives any kind of machine;

also, a steam-powered railroad locomotive

stern the back end of a boat or a ship

subway an underground passage used by trains

terminal a station for passengers using some type of transportation, such as an airplane or train

towrope a rope attached to a vehicle, allowing it to be pulled by another vehicle

yacht a popular type of pleasure boat

1882 Attalla, Alabama, is the first American city to use electric street lights

1892 Adoph Friedrich Erdmann von Menzel paints *On a Journey to Beautiful Countryside* (pp. 14–17)

1893 Fred Pansing paints *Leading the Fleet into New York Harbor* (pp. 48–49)

1900

c. 1910–20 Christiaan Pieter Snijders paints *Ludgate Hill* (pp. 18–21)

1903 Orville and Wilbur Wright fly the first pilot-controlled aircraft for 120 feet (36.5 m) at Kitty Hawk, North Carolina

1918 François Flameng paints *The Airfield* (pp. 52–55)

1927 Aviator Charles Lindbergh makes the first solo transatlantic airplane flight

1928 John Sloan paints *The Sixth Avenue Elevated at Third Street* (pp. 22–25)

1932–33 Diego Rivera paints *The Detroit Industry Murals* (pp. 26–29)

1964 Japan introduces the first high-speed "bullet trains," running at about 125 miles (200 km) per hour

c. 1944 C. C. Turner paints *Glider Training* (pp. 54–55)

1969 The first true wide-body airliners come into service

1981 NASA launches the first space shuttle, possibly the beginning of a new era of transportation—travel into outer space

1994 Eurostar train services provide an undersea rail link between England and France

2000

1999 Jiro Osuga paints *Flight* (pp. 56–59)

FURTHER READING

Coiley, J. *Train.* New York: Dorling Kindersley, 2000.

Herbst, Judith. *The History of Transportation* (Major Inventions Through History series). Minneapolis: Twenty-First Century Books, 2006.

Hynson, Colin. *A History of Railroads.* Milwaukee: Gareth Stevens Publishers, 2006.

Lavery, Brian. *Ship: 5,000 Years of Maritime Adventure.* New York: Dorling Kindersley/National Maritime Museum/Smithsonian, 2004.

Rinard, Judith. *The Book of Flight: The Smithsonian National Air and Space Museum.* Willowdale, ON: Firefly Books, 2001.

Sandler, Martin W. *Transportation in America.* 6 vols. Oxford: Oxford University Press, 2003–2004.

Sutton, Richard and Baquedano, Elizabeth. *Car.* New York: Dorling Kindersley, 2005.

Williams, Harriet. *Road and Rail Transportation* (History of Inventions series). New York: Facts on File, 2004.

WEBSITES

History of Transportation
www.centennialofflight.gov
Excellent site exploring the history and development of all aspects of aviation since the Wright Brothers

www.century-of-flight.net
Another site exploring the history and development of aviation since the beginning

www.cruise-charter.net/history-of-sailing/
Provides a history of sailing, starting with the ancient Egyptians, and gives information on the different types of vessels used to travel the seas

www.imh.org/imh/exh1.html
"The International Museum of the Horse" is a detailed historical site on horses and horse-riding since prehistoric times

www.nasm.si.edu/education/onlinelearning.cfm
An exciting website sponsored by the Smithsonian Air and Space Museum, providing a variety of online activities on aviation and spaceflight

www.nycsubway.org
Fascinating site on public transportation in New York City, including information on the old elevated lines

www.pedalinghistory.com
Informative and entertaining site on the history of the bicycle

www.sdrm.org/history/
Pacific Southwest Railroad Museum website, with information on general railroad history as well as Californian trains, and good links to other railroad sites

Artwork about Transportation
www.metmuseum.org
The Metropolitan Museum of Art, New York

www.nmm.ac.uk
The National Maritime Museum, Greenwich, England

www.americanart.si.edu/collections/index.cfm
The Smithsonian Museum of American Art, Washington, DC

Index

A

accidents, 13, 21, 25, 36, 38
air traffic control, 58
airplanes, 50–59
    aircraft industry, 56
    jet aircraft, 50, 55, 56
    military planes, 51, 54–55
    passenger planes, 50, 53, 56–59.
    See also flying boats; gliders
airport security, 58
airport terminals, 56–59
anchors, 46
armies, 51
assembly lines, 27–29
automobiles, 18, 25, 26–29

B

Baedeker, Karl, 17
balloons, hot-air, 50
Baltimore and Ohio Railroad, 10
barges, 39
Barnet Fair, England, 6, 7
battles, maritime, 48, 49
bicycles, 4, 20
Blériot, Louis, 51
boats, 30, 31, 34, 35, 39, 40, 43, 44–47
boilers, steam, 13, 36
bombers, Dakota, 55
bombing raids, 54
Bricker, Mead, 28
buses, 18, 21

C

Canaletto, 32–33, 34
canals, 34, 35
cars. See automobiles
chocks, 53
Civil War, American, 10, 44
cockpits, airplane, 55
conductors, railroad, 17
Confederacy, 10
Crimean War, 42
Cunard line, 43, 48

D

Daedalus, 50
Darling, Grace, 36
Detroit, MI, 26–27

E

electricity, 24, 29
engine drivers, 12
engines
    gasoline engines, 29
    jet engines, 54, 55
    propeller-driven, 55
    steam engines, 13, 31, 36, 38
England, 18, 30, 32, 36. See also Great Britain
Erie Railway, 5
Europe, 14, 16, 17, 22, 30, 31, 32, 38

F

ferries, 31, 39
fishing, 44, 46, 47
flags, 39, 48
Flameng, François, 52, 53
flying boats, 56
flying suits, 53
Ford, Henry, 26, 28, 29
Ford cars, 26–29
Forfarshire, SS, 36–37, 38
freight, 35, 39

G

Garros, Roland, 52
gliders, 54, 55
gondolas, 34
Great Britain, 6, 18, 20, 21, 38, 39, 42, 43, 51, 55. See also England; Scotland
guns (on ships), 49

H

harbors, 32–33, 36, 48
Hartsfield Airport, Atlanta, 59
Heathrow Airport, London, 56
Herring, Sr., John Frederick, 6, 7

Homer, Winslow, 44–45
horses, 4–9
    horse-drawn vehicles, 4, 5, 7, 18, 21
    horse fairs, 6–7
    horse riding, 8–9
    workhorses, 20
horseshoes, 8
Hudson River, 31

I

Icarus, 50
immigrants, 31
Iowa, 18
Iowa (battleship), 48, 49

K

Karger, Carl, 10–11
Kitty Hawk, NC, 50

L

Le Mans, France, 51
Leonardo da Vinci, 50
lifeboats, 40, 43
lighting, 12, 24
Lindbergh, Charles, 51
Lloyd's List, 42
locomotives, 10, 12, 13. See also trains
London, England, 6, 18, 20, 21, 22, 40, 51, 56
Ludgate Hill, London, 18, 19

M

mail deliveries, 5
Manhattan, 22, 31
maritime accidents, 36, 38
Massachusetts, 46, 47
Mayflower, the, 31
Menzel, Adolph von, 14–15
Model T Ford, 26, 29

N

navies, 43, 48
navigational aids, 32, 43, 54

New York City, 5, 21, 22, 24, 30, 48, 49
New York, USS, 48, 49
North America, 4, 10, 20, 22, 31. See also United States

O

Ohio, 58
oil lamps, 12
Osuga, Jiro, 56–57

P

paddle-steamers, 31, 36, 38
Pansing, Fred, 48, 49
Paris, France, 8–9, 21, 22, 50
Pilgrims, the, 30
pilots, 53
    fighter pilots, 52
police officers, 18
porters, railroad, 12
posters, travel, 5
public transportation, 25

R

railroads, 5, 20, 22–25
    railroad accidents, 13
    railroad bridges, 20
    railroad stations, 10–13
    railroad travel, 10–17. See also trains
Renoir, Pierre Auguste, 8, 9
rigging, 42
River Rouge, Detroit, 26
Rivera, Diego, 26–27, 28
roads, 18–21
    road traffic accidents, 21, 25
    road traffic signals, 21
Rome, ancient, 32

S

sailboats, 44–47
sails, 42, 47
Santiago de Cuba, Battle of, 48, 49
Scotland, 16

PICTURE CREDITS

Abbreviations:
T=Top; M=Middle; B=Bottom;
R=Right; L=Left

1 Detail from *Sixth Avenue Elevated at Third Street*, 1928 (oil on canvas), by John Sloan, (1871–11), Whitney Museum of American Art, New York on pages 22–23. **2** Detail from *The American Railway Scene at Hornellsville, Erie Railway* on page 5. **3** Detail from *Breezing Up (A Fair Wind)*, 1873–1876 (oil on canvas) by Winslow Homer/Gift of the W. L. and May T. Mellon Foundation on pages 44–46, ML; Detail from *The American Railway Scene at Hornellsville, Erie Railway* on page 5, T; Detail from *Ludgate Hill* by C. P. Snijders on page 19, TR; Detail from *The Airfield, 1918* by Francois Flameng on pages 52, BR. **4** *Blanche d'Antigny (1870–74) and her Velocipede* (oil on canvas) by Betinet, (19th century)/Musee de l'Ile de France, Sceaux, France/Lauros/Giraudon/The Bridgeman Art Library. **5** *Why the Mail was Late* (oil on canvas) by Berninghaus, Oscar Edward (1874–1952)/Thomas Gilcrease Institute, Tulsa, Oklahoma/courtesy Barbara B. Brenner/The Bridgeman Art Library; *The American Railway Scene at Hornellsville, Erie Railway* (print, 1874) Currier, N. (1813–88) and Ives, J. M. (1824–95)/Private Collection/The Bridgeman Art Library, BR. **6** *Barnet Fair*, by John Frederick Herring Sr. (1795–1865), © Harrogate Museums and Art Gallery, North Yorkshire/The Bridgeman Art Library. **7** Details from *Barnet Fair* on page, 6. **8** Details from *Horsewoman in the Bois de Boulogne* on page 9. **9** *Horsewoman in the Bois de Boulogne, 1873* (oil on canvas) by Pierre Auguste Renoir, (1841–1919)/Hamburger Kunsthalle,

Hamburg, Germany/The Bridgeman Art Library. **10–11** *Nordwest Bahnhof, Vienna, 1875* by Carl Karger, (1848–1913)/Osterreichische Galerie Belvedere, Vienna, Austria/The Bridgeman Art Library. **12–13** Details from *Nordwest Bahnhof, Vienna* on pages 10–11. **14–15** *On a Journey to Beautiful Countryside, 1892* (gouache on paper) by Adolph Freidrich Erdmann von Menzel, (1815–1905) Hamburg Kunstalle, Hamburg/The Bridgeman Art Library. **16–17** Details from *On a Journey to Beautiful Countryside* on pages 14–15. **18** Details from *Ludgate Hill* on page 19. **19** *Ludgate Hill* by C. P. Snijders/Private Collection/The Bridgeman Art Library. **20–21** Details from *Ludgate Hill* on page 19. **22–23** *Sixth Avenue Elevated at Third Street, 1928* (oil on canvas), John Sloan, (1871–1951)/Whitney Museum of American Art, New York. **24–25** Details from *Sixth Avenue Elevated at Third Street, 1928* on pages 22–23. **26–27** *Detroit Industry, South Wall, 1932–1933* by Diego M Rivera/Gift of Edsel B. Ford/Photograph © 2001 The Detroit Institute of Arts, Michigan, USA. **28–29** Details from *Detroit Industry, South Wall, 1932–33* on pages 26–27. **30** *Sign for the Marangoni Family of shipbuilders*, Venetian, 1517 (oil on panel) by Italian School, (16th century) Museo Correr, Venice/Giraudon/The Bridgeman Art Library. **31** *Steamship Syracuse, 1857* (oil on canvas) by Bard, James (1815–97) © Peabody Essex Museum, Salem, Massachusetts, USA/The Bridgeman Art Library, T; **31** *Wall Street, Ferry Ship* (oil on canvas) by Cooper, Colin Campbell (1856–1937)/Private Collection/David Findlay Jr, Fine Art, NYC, USA/The Bridgeman Art Library,

B. **32–33** *The Riva Degli Schiavoni: A view of Venice looking west with St. Mark's, the Dooge's Palace, and Santa Maria della Salute in the background,* 1736 (oil on canvas) Antonio Canaletto, (1697-1768) © The Trustees of Sir John Soane's Museum, 13 Lincoln's Inn Fields, London. **34–35** Details from *The Riva Degli Schiavoni*: on pages 32–33. **36–37** SS Forfarshire *Leaving Hull on her Last Voyage* (oil on canvas) John Ward, (1798–1849)/© Ferens Art Gallery, Hull City Museum and Art Galleries/The Bridgeman Art Library. **38–39** Details from SS Forfarshire *Leaving Hull on her Last Voyage* on pages 36–37. **40–41** *The Last Evening, 1873* (oil on canvas) by James Jacques Josepg Tissot, (1836–1902)/© Guildhall Art Gallery, City of London/The Bridgeman Art Library. **42–43** Details from *The Last Evening, 1873* on pages 40–41. **44–45** *Breezing Up (A Fair Wind), 1873–76* (oil on canvas) Winslow Homer/Gift of the W. L. and May T. Mellon Foundation/National Gallery of Art, Washington, USA. **46–47** Details from *Breezing Up (A Fair Wind)* on pages 44–45. 48ML Detail from *Naval Parade, held in honor of Commander George Dewey (1837-1917)* 1898 on pages 48–49T. **48–49** *Naval Parade, held in honor of Commander George Dewey (1837-1917)* 1898 (oil on canvas by Fred Pansing, (1854–1912) © Museum of the City of New York, USA/The Bridgeman Art Library. **49** Details from *Naval Parade, held in honor of Commander George Dewey (1837-1917)* 1898. **50** *Page of text and sketches for a flying machine, c.1480,* pen and ink on paper, by Leonardo da Vinci (1452–1519) Ms. B f.83v/ Bibliotheque de l'Institute de France, Paris/Giraudon/The Bridgeman Art Library. **51** *The First Flight of the Wright Brothers at Kitty Hawk, North Carolina, 1903,* from 'Histoire

d'Aviation' by Rene Chambe, 1949 (color litho) by Albert Brenet, (1903–81)/Private Collection/The Bridgeman Art Library, T. **51** *For Every Fighter a Woman Worker* World War I YWCA propaganda poster by Adolph Treidler, (1846–1905) (after) Victoria & Albert Museum, London, UK/The Bridgeman Art Library, B. **52** *The Airfield, 1918* (w/c on paper) by Francois Flameng, (1856–1923)/ Musee de l'Armee, Paris/The Bridgeman Art Library. **53** Details from *The Airfield, 1918* on page 52. **54** *Glider Training, c.1944* (oil on canvas) by C. C. Turner, (20th Century)/© Canadian War Museum, Ottawa, Canada/The Bridgeman Art Library. **55** Details from *Glider Training, c.1944* on page 54. **56–57** *Flight, 1999* (oil and acrylic on canvas) by Jiro Osuga, courtesy of Flowers, London/The Bridgeman Art Library. **58–59** Details *from Flight, 1999* on pages 56–57.

Front cover: Detail from *Glider Training, c.1944* (oil on canvas) by C.C. Turner, (20th Century)/© Canadian War Museum, Ottawa, Canada/The Bridgeman Art Library.
Back cover: *The Riva Degli Schiavoni: A view of Venice looking west with St. Mark's, the Dooge's Palace and Santa Maria della Salute in the background,* 1736 (oil on canvas) Antonio Canaletto, (1697-1768) © The Trustees of Sir John Soane's Museum, 13 Lincoln's Inn Fields, London, L. Detail from *Nordwest Bahnhof, Vienna, 1875* by Carl Karger, (1848–1913)/Osterreichische Galerie Belvedere, Vienna, Austria/The Bridgeman Art Library.
Background image:
Fabric/M.Angelo/Corbis.